Chicken Soup

Chicken Soup

and other medical matters

cartoons by S. Harris

Foreword by Willard R. Espy

WILLIAM KAUFMANN, INC.   LOS ALTOS, CALIFORNIA

The individual cartoons in this book have been previously published
and copyrighted by:

*American Medical News, American Scientist, Environment,
Chicago Tribune, Chronicle of Higher Education, Cavalier,
Changing Times, The Critic, Johns Hopkins Magazine,
Medical Economics, Medical World News, Medical
Tribune, Playboy, Private Practice, Psychiatric News,
Saturday Evening Post, Saturday Review, Wall Street
Journal, Washington Star, Washingtonian.*

Cartoons from *Playboy* appear on pages 12, 30, 41, 63, 75,
87, 98.

The cartoons have been reprinted with permission, and our thanks
go to all the above publications.

ISBN 0-913232-75-0   ISBN 0-913232-74-2 pbk.

Printed in the United States of America

FOREWORD

A number of my friends are writers, artists, or cartoonists.

By and large, writers depress me. When drunk, they endlessly trace in their navels the contours of a relentlessly imperfect universe. When sober, they brood over not being drunk.

Artists, again speaking in general, drink for pleasure; when not drinking, they are sleeping it off. My only complaint against artists is that they tend to begrudge lending out their models.

But my favorite friends are cartoonists. Like Christian in *Pilgrim's Progress,* they have successfully crossed the Slough of Despond and the Valley of the Shadow of Death. They have slain the Giant Despair. They have passed over, and all the trumpets have sounded for them on the other side.

I mean, they are the Good Guys.

Writers are on firm ground about the flaws of the universe. Artists are entirely within their rights to keep their models to themselves. But cartoonists take the stuff of hopelessness and tears—despair itself, the ultimate, ineluctable defeat—and make us laugh.

The medical treatise that follows is an example. Medicine is but a pathetic little dam of sand, raised with a child's shovel against the onrushing tide of oblivion. Laughable, to be sure; but not funny. Yet a great cartoonist like Sidney Harris makes even mortality hilarious.

As when a masked woman holds up a sperm bank at the point of a gun.

Or a patient asks a doctor who arrives with a guinea pig in a cage, "You mean you're going to test it on a guinea pig *now*?"

They tell me, Sidney, that you have made and sold some 10,000 drawings. For each and all of them, my thanks.

Will you see to it, when my time comes, that I have this book by my hospital bed? It would be nice to die laughing.

Willard R. Espy

"It only hurts when I sneeze."

"This sugar substitute is perfect except for one thing. It's salty."

S. Harris

"... and seven years ago I donated
one of my kidneys to him. I want it back."

3

"Apparently some of the additives cause a nerve disorder, but some of the other additives cure it."

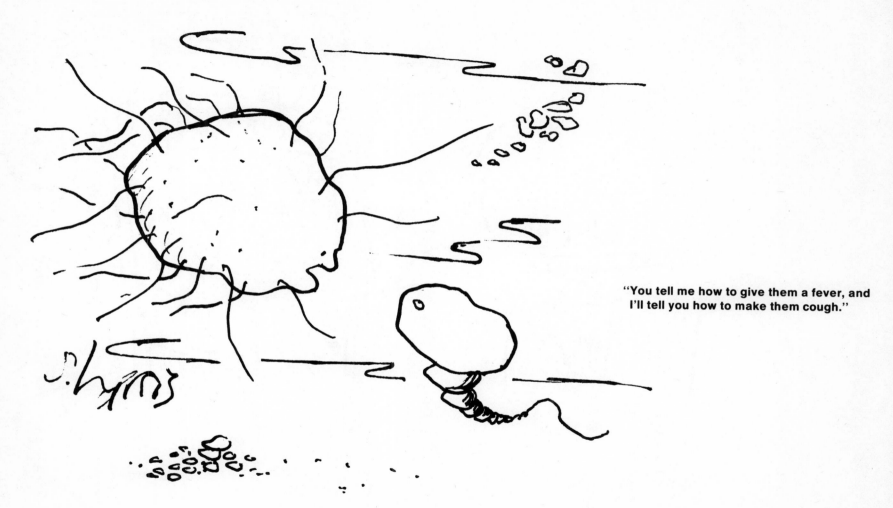

"You tell me how to give them a fever, and I'll tell you how to make them cough."

5

"I'm always like this, and my family was wondering if you could prescribe a mild depressant."

7

"After seeing the midwife so many
years, he ran off with her."

"What's wrong with white mice and guinea pigs?"

9

"Stick to it. There's a future in cryogenics."

10

"But socialized medicine may pave the way for a *really* major breakthrough—socialized liquor."

"It was just a fun transplant.
   You got his heart, he got yours."

"It's all right if you sing to yourself. Why is it peculiar if you *talk* to yourself?"

"It must be acupuncture!
My toothache is gone."

15

"More hot water!"

"It cures it in chickens;
it causes it in mice."

17

"There's another hereditary disease that runs in the royal family. Your grandfather was a stubborn fool, your father was a stubborn fool, and *you* are a stubborn fool."

"It won't be long now—
I'm in my 18th month."

"You're not making it any
easier for either of us."

20

"Son, I hear you failed genetics!"

21

" 'Hackley's Syndrome'? But Dr. Grottmark
said it was 'Grottmark's Syndrome.' "

"You mean you're going to test
it on a guinea pig *now*?"

"The answer is politics. In your manic state you can go out campaigning, and in your depressive state you can stay in the office."

"What I'd really like to do, of course, is just find a cure for the common plague."

"That lumbago you just got rid of—
you gave it to me!"

"Who called me a quack?"

"Dr. Frobisher's office—gesundheit."

"But I take the pill every time I become pregnant, and it doesn't help."

S. Marris

"You don't like it and I don't like it, but the FCC likes it."

"It's very inflamed. Why don't you take
a vow of silence for a few days?"

"I think we can rule out stress."

"I can understand my mother and my first-grade teacher being there, but there's also a TV announcer who does dog food commercials and a second-string catcher for the Detroit Tigers."

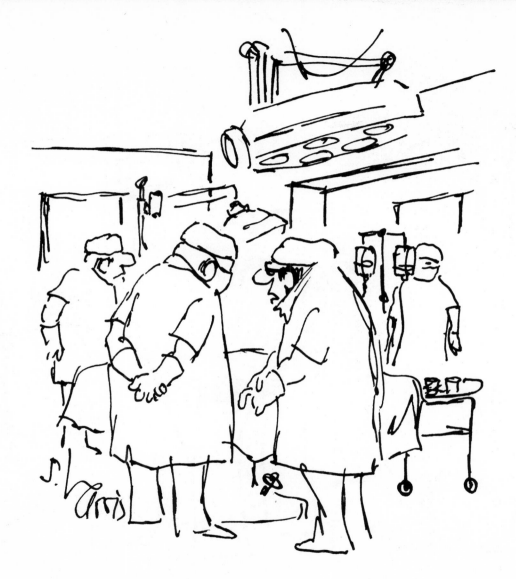

'We'll only do 72% of it, since it's been reported that 28% of all surgery is unnecessary.''

"To think I used to complain about making house calls!"

"What it is is a giant kidney."

"Nonsense! You don't use diathermy for that. You use a whirlpool bath."

"A woman obsetrician! What do women know about that sort of thing?"

"There's an inspector here from the Board of Health who would like to see the chicken soup."

"Just for kicks, let's come up with something that has a good side effect."

"... sodium phosphate, di-glycerides, BHT. Warning: The Surgeon General has determined that eating is dangerous to your health."

"What's so good about it?
It's my blood pressure."

44

"This is all just a front.
Actually, I'm a faith healer."

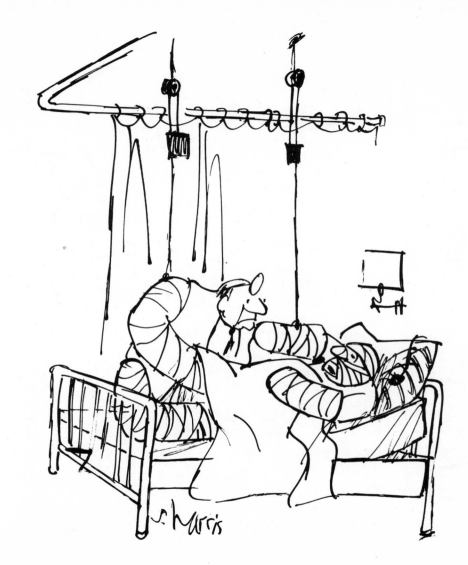

"You call all this a *side-effect*?"

"I believe I have a new approach to psychotherapy, but, like everything else, the FDA tells me it first has to be tested on mice."

"Just between you and me,
do you really cause warts?"

48

"Run, Spot, run."

"It's partly glandular and
partly 8,500 calories per day."

50

"At present, my son and I are extremely interested in genetics and heredity."

"I'd say it's a fungal infection."

"He claims to be a specialist, but
I think he just has a one-track mind."

54

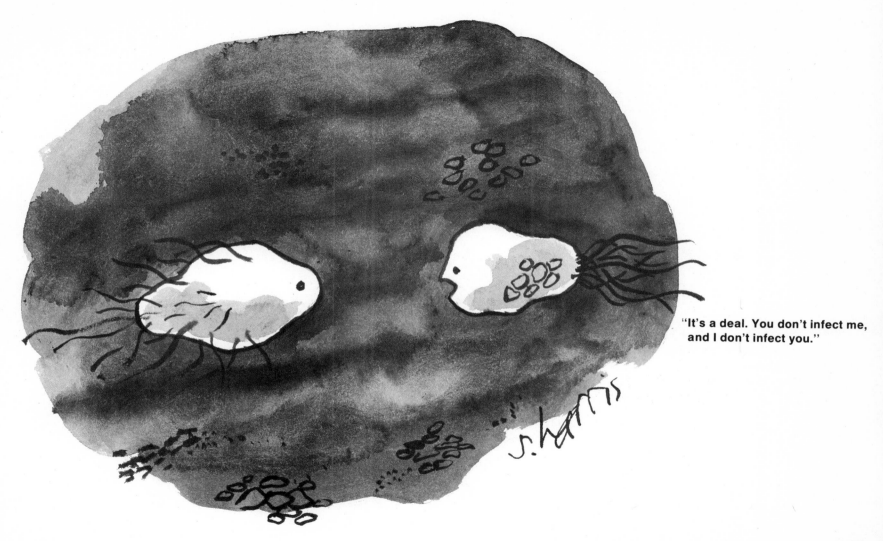

"It's a deal. You don't infect me,
and I don't infect you."

"Sure it's a nuisance to run home
for every meal; but it's either that
or the Chinese-restaurant syndrome."

"Your ear trouble is caused by loud noises in the air, your nose trouble is caused by funny smells in the air, and your throat trouble is caused by strange particles in the air."

'Since we got up off all fours I've
been having these low back pains.''

"Well, you see, I went to one of those progressive medical schools with no formal classes or credits and the students plan their own course of study—so I never learned anything about the lungs and breathing and all that."

"I feel better today too, but around here I've learned not to be too optimistic."

"It was more of a *'triple*-blind' test. The patients didn't know which ones were getting the real drug, the doctors didn't know, and, I'm afraid nobody knew."

"A heart transplant isn't worth much if he doesn't look good—let's give him a hair transplant, too."

63

"He says he makes housecalls, and he'll be over as soon as he gets his horse back from the blacksmith."

"Hot compresses! Won't *cold* compresses do?"

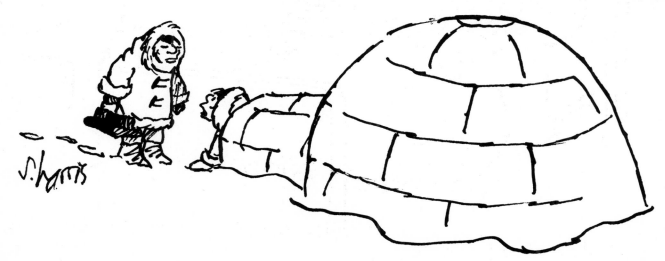

'The beauty of this pitch is that it can be thrown with a sore arm, charley horse, trick knee, and bone chips in the heel.''

"He claims it's not an upper respiratory infection—it's a lower respiratory infection. In his foot."

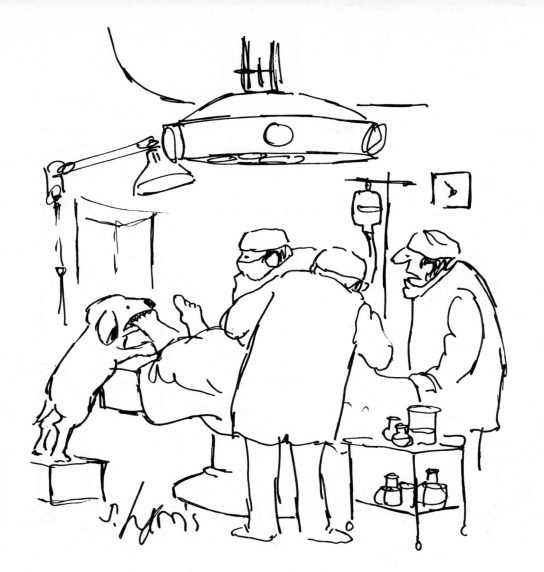

"Malpractice? No—it's not *our* dog."

"What do you mean 'don't expect miracles'?
Why *shouldn't* I expect miracles?"

"Looks like a virus."

"He has my nose and Fred's postnasal drip."

"Congratulations—You're the first victim of recombinant DNA.'

"Gold and silver from base metals is OK, but what I'm trying to transmute is angelica root, mugwort and tincture of marigold into an effective aphrodisiac."

"I can't complain. Last week
they had me on martinis."

"Enough acupuncture—
get me a couple of aspirin."

"I can't remember the last time I
   treated a case of amnesia, and I can't even
   remember if I ever did treat one."

"Let me put it this way: you're an addict, and your grocer is a pusher."

"Dr. Krantz referred you to me? I was going to refer you to Dr. Krantz."

"Remember his weakness is a
pulled tendon, so keep it as high as your
bursitis will let you, but take it easy with
your fast ball because of my bone chips."

"But you can't sue me for malpractice. I'm not a doctor!"

"You're giving me an ulcer!"

84

"The pituitary transplant was a complete success, and you will be going home soon. However, I want you to call me at the first sign of a strong desire to swing from trees and devour bananas."

"Of course I'm nervous.
I'm double parked."

"I have some bad news. Your health plan doesn't cover bandages."

"Walk, damn it!"

"Of course I've become more mature since you started treating me. You've been at it since I was 14 years old."

"He's a very sick elephant."

"One reason this condition is so hard to cure is that it's caused by one of the *teeniest* viruses."

"Is there another doctor in the house?
He wants a second opinion."

"You'd like to get a second opinion?
I'll give you a second opinion."

"So I told the doctor I'm a major league baseball player and I don't have any *time* to get out in the sunshine."

"As a matter of fact, I have the heart of a 30-year-old woman."

95

"Don't worry. Soon there'll be
drugs that'll keep you alive far beyond
99 years and a day."

"But why on earth, Mr. Dressen, would you want a *twelfth* opinion?"

"How can we *prevent* pregnancy? We don't even know what *causes* it."

98

"If you want fiber, Madame,
I suggest you eat the menu."

99

"In the off-season I generally do some hunting and fishing, help out in my father's auto showroom, have knee surgery, and work out in my hometown youth center."

"Apparently, Mr. Fradkin,
evolution is a two-way street."

About the Artist

Turning his back on reality, S. Harris claims his ambition hasn't changed in decades. He still wants to play center field for his hometown team, the Brooklyn Dodgers. While waiting for this big break, he rides his bike, continues a running battle with the mysteries of playing the piano, gives an occasional lecture attempting to explain his work, and, in his spare time, draws cartoons.

His grandfather, who did a great deal of walking as he went from job to job cleaning store windows in New York City, would, at the end of a hard week, soak his tired feet in a tub of hot liquid. Harris claims the rest of this book is fiction.

His previous cartoon collections are: 'So Far, So Good (Playboy Press, 1971), 'Pardon Me, Miss' (Dell Publishing Co., 1973) and 'What's So Funny about Science?' (William Kaufmann, Inc., 1977).